I AM NAKIA

…

UNAPOLOGETICALLY

NAKIA MOODY

I AM NAKIA...UNAPOLOGETICALLY
By Nakia Moody

Copyright © by Nakia Moody

Cover Design by Izii_Designer (via Fiverr)

ISBN: 978-0-578-27200-9

Printed in the United States of America

I'm writing this about a strong black woman!

Nakia is a single mom of four. The way she handles herself is unbelievable. We've been friends for 10 years. Nakia is a solid friend that you can count on. She is the real definition of a friend!

Over the years I have watched her grow/glow into a beautiful woman and mother. With every hurdle that comes up, she finds a way to master that big jump. To say I'm proud is an understatement. To watch her build businesses for her family and herself, I am happy to be here to witness greatness and to continue to watch this beautiful flower bloom.

She is a great motivator and influential person to be around. With that being said, I'm super proud of my friend!

Lynette Moore

From the day you came home from the hospital, as your Big
Sister, I knew I had to be your protector.
I can remember the times you were at my house babysitting
and making sure my girls had their hair done. Fast forward
to the present time, and I'm in awe watching you master
your craft and becoming a business owner.
It was always my pleasure to spoil you with love and
affection. I will cherish all the good times we've spent
together – the laughs, the cries, and being my ride. Life
hasn't always been easy for you, but you have always pressed
forward. For that, I admire your strength and your resilience.
I love you to life. I will always be your biggest fan.

Toya Jan

My beautiful daughter, Nakia Moody…

I have watched you grow up and walking in your purpose. I am ever so proud to see you flourish.

Remember to always keep God first.

I love you – don't let anyone destroy your dreams!

Mom

I am proud to say that the progress of the young Queen Nakia Moody is incredible. Since working with her, she has progressed in branding, networking, and more. And she continues to strive to become better.

Melvin Johnson

Founder, Unapologetic Podcast, LLC

DEDICATION

I dedicate this book to Melvin Jr., Braydon, Nakayla, and Nason. I want to apologize for being ill prepared prior to the birth of all four of you into this world. I knew I wanted to be an exceptional mother to the four of you, and I must admit that I failed miserably. Despite my failures, you don't have to make the same mistakes. I created this book as a blueprint to assist you with ushering you into the truth I've never spoken about. This is my written love letter to the four of you because life is short, but my words shall abide if you pick up this book.

My intentions were pure, but my motivation was self-serving. In my attempts to be a better mother, I failed you all. I allowed toxic relationships, trauma, the opinions of others, and the things that I saw cause my boat to capsize. When you entered the world, my heart was filled with bitterness, resentment, and a desire to give you everything that I never received.

While you are a child examining the adults around you, you guys think to yourselves, I will NOT be like them. You all have so many dreams, aspirations, and an indomitable spirit. Please hold tight to them, and please never allow water to pour into your boat. Keep God first in all that you do.

Melvin (My Heartbeat), I resented you for being ungrateful, but you didn't have a measuring stick to even know you were being ungrateful. I had spoiled you, and I became angry and felt used. I thank you for packing your bags and abandoning me for your dad. you saved my life.

Thank you for loving me enough to allow me to hit rock bottom. Thank you for giving me time alone to heal as a woman. Thank you for allowing me to heal in private so that my process did not cause you any more trauma in the long run. Thank you for forgiving me for my shortcomings. Thank you for loving me unconditionally. Thank you for choosing me as a vessel for your entry into this world. Thank you for coming back to me.

Love Always,

MOM

CONTENTS

ACKNOWLEDGMENTS

I have to start by thanking God, who is the head of my life, for loving me and never giving up on me despite all things. I want to mention that if it had not been for God's grace and mercy, I would not be here today.

I would like to thank Katrina Wells, who first made it possible for me to become an author - something I never dreamed would happen.

I would not have been able to get this book done without the continuous support and vision of my editor, Shanika Carter of The Write Flow & Vibe, with enormous skill, warmth, and precision.

I thank all who in one way or another contributed to this book rather emotionally and physically:

I want to thank my children's fathers. You guys made my life a living hell. I was damaged for so many years behind your hurt and unwillingness to heal.

I thank you for the hell you fellas put me through. I thank you for abandoning your children and more so turning them against me. Without the physical, mental, and emotional abuse, I wouldn't have counted on God! I would have counted God out. Thanks for telling me I wasn't good enough. I was able to let God show me that I am enough!

Thank you for dragging my name through hell and back. I was able to let God make you my footstool. Thank you for every time you hit me in my face to destroy my image. It allowed God to make my image as an 18-year-old at the age of 35. Thanks for leaving your kid behind selfishly. Now I can teach them all good things.

Thanks for leaving me with your responsibilities. It made me stronger than

I ever thought. It allowed me to see that God is a "Father to the Fatherless". I depend on him to see us through.

Thank you for calling me every name but Nakia. Now I know I am "QUEEN" – a daughter of King Jesus.

I also want to thank every single person who ever says, "You have to read this book!" to a friend. I pray this book gets into the hands of readers who may need to hear my story.

Lastly, Lord thank you for a praying mother. Those prayers and her tremendous amount of faith in God has saved me knowingly and unknowingly.

God Bless!

PROLOGUE

This book starts with a fairly straightforward question – have you lowered your value? Most of us have lowered our value based on the treatment we have experienced from others. I'm here to tell you, their words have no power over you. Speak life into yourself. I want you to find your voice in this season. You have been overwhelmed for too long and have lost sight of who you are for too long. I AM –UNAPOLOGETIC. I declare healing and restoration, do you?

As children, we were conditioned by fairytales that told us Prince Charming would show up to rescue us. For many of us, Prince Charming never showed up. And I unknowingly, and unaware of the road ahead of me, was affected by his absence and was not ready for the damage it would cause.

I suffered abuse in many ways: verbally, physically, emotionally, and mentally. I was left to care for four children without any reliable resources with no father figure; exposed to sex; set back; slandered. I was gullible and naive. I had a lack of knowledge about this thing called life. It left me with resentment that would damage me for life, at least I thought it would until Prince Charming showed up to me as Jesus Christ. He became a way maker, door opener, and lover of my soul. He had been waiting on me to walk into my destiny.

I had to learn the hard way that people will express their desire to be loved but their actions may oppose the words they have spoken. I had to learn and know that I was not only beautiful on the outside but also beautiful on the inside even more. I have a heart of gold that has led me to attract narcissistic men; lovers of cleaning you out of everything with no remorse. I have been kind to people, and they have taken my kindness for weakness. I realize I'm miserable because I refused to love myself – apologetically! Never again.

I used to give people chance after chance, but some people must grow up and outside of your presence. I now understand boundaries. I have no hard feelings and I wish you well, but I don't have the time to wait on someone to heal and be made whole. Please don't allow others to tear you down, and if you have never heard it from another human being, I want you to know you are beautiful and worthy of so much. Add some positive affirmations to your life:

I am loved, I am beautiful, I am worthy, I am capable. Repeat!

"Father of the fatherless and protector of the widows, is God in his holy habitation" - Psalm 68:5

I AM - A FATHERLESS CHILD

"Dad!

Why have you never taught me how a man is supposed to treat a woman, huh? Why did you do every woman who crossed your path horrible? Why didn't you ever tell your baby girl she was beautiful? Why did you never keep your word that I trusted in? Why did you make me feel I couldn't be loved or good enough because I was heavier than other girls? Why did you use me the majority of my life? Why wouldn't you teach me how to drive? Why do you treat my siblings better than me? Why did you always take credit for things I had no choice but to do on my own? Why didn't you protect me from abusive relationships? Why don't you love me? What made me not be good enough to be your child? Why would you tell me sometimes that a man has to put his hands on you? Why would you leave me to go look for love in a man? A man who treated me like a piece of shit? Like you do everyone, huh? Why don't you love or cherish your grandchildren? Why don't you help your kids when they reach out for you? What is it about my brother that you cherish more than us? Why did you take me with you to each lady's house where you had sex? Why did you used to leave me at school every day? Why didn't you ever come to watch me perform in our youth talent shows? Why didn't you support anything I ever did? Why haven't I seen you not even one of the three times I've graduated? Why didn't you ever come to your grandson's football games? Why do you only come around to look or look like you're involved? Why did you leave my mother so bitter that she couldn't love me? Why won't you grow up? What's stopping you from growing up? Why don't you want to see me happy? Why does knowing when I'm struggling and going through things make you smile?

Why did you treat your own mother like shit? What do you know about why my granny's missing? Why do you use and disregard your siblings? Why are you a user? Why do you lie to my kids?

Why don't you spend time with your grandkids?

Honor your mother and father?

Dad, I hate the way you talk! I hate how ignorant you are and how you're okay staying stuck in your ways. I hate how selfish you are! I hate how you are okay with fucking over anybody as long as it benefits you! I hate how stupidly you think! I hate how you don't have respect. I hate you treat me like shit! I hate you never taught me anything. I hate you for giving me body and self-hate issues. I hate you never taught me how a man is supposed to treat me. I hate you left at the times I needed you most. I hate how someone else was always more important than me. I hate you!"

G od has always been my father, even in the absence of my earthly father. From as early as I can remember, my dad always just came and went as he pleased. Even when he was out doing things that no child should ever witness her dad doing, it was all about him and what he wanted.

I never witnessed the history of my dad and my mom, but I've always heard the stories and believed what I have been told. I witnessed the tail end of their relationship, what I call a waste of time on my mother's behalf. After going through what I've been through as an adult woman who thought she was in love, that is how I see it. But the wants of the heart are sickening. These wants have you dealing with things that make you cringe when you think back later down the line.

I was naive to many things going on in the world when I was younger, because I was sheltered. I remember my dad always being in the streets and juggling women. And many times, I was right along for the ride. He would take me to the different houses of these women, watching as each woman cooked for him, gave him money, and did anything else he wanted. He and these women would leave me on the couch to watch television and disappear for hours in the room. I now realize that he left me sitting there so he could go have sex with them. At times, he would drop me off with the women and wouldn't come back to get me. Sometimes I would even miss school. I even remember days being left at school because he would be too busy with his women and forget to pick me up. He would always tell me that he loved me and say that it would never happen again, but of course it did. And because I believed him each time, it hurt even more.

I always felt I was never good enough for my dad. He would spend more time with my brothers and sisters, who had a different father, than he would with me. He even spent time with the children of the women he was seeing. He acted as if I wasn't there. I would wait for hours upon hours for him to pick me up, staring out the window looking at every car that passed, but he never showed up. As a father, how can you tell a child that you are coming to get them but never show up? As a father, how can you have a child sitting and waiting for you when you have no intentions of ever showing up? Even worse, how can you see your child and then hide from them?

I remember going to the candy store one day on my way home from school as a kid. As my friend and I approached the store, I could see my dad inside. I got so excited and rushed into the store only to find him gone. He was nowhere to be found, but I knew that I had seen him. He had hidden from me. My own father went and hid from me, so he didn't have to see me. This type of behavior made me feel as if he hated me, and I couldn't figure out what I did for him to react to me like this, so I cried all the way home. I bottled it all up. I didn't even tell my mom when I got home, but I did speak to God.

I asked God why I had to have the father that I did who did not show up to graduations, conferences, talent shows or anything for me. The hurt caused by this toxic relationship led me to toxic relationships with other men in my life. I accepted the love they decided they wanted to give which was based on lies, deceit, and repeated apologies. Because I forgave my dad time after time, that's what I always did with these men – forgive them time after time for the fuckedup shit that they did to me. How could I grow up to be confident when most of the hurt I received by men came from how I felt about myself around my dad?

I once told my dad that I would never get a boyfriend because of the way that I looked, because my dad told me that I didn't look like the smaller girls. He said I was too big for anyone to want me, and I believed him. That was the beginning of my self-hate. This only became worse when my dad had a biracial child, who he loved and doted on, so much that you would have thought that he gave birth to him. Imagine how that made me feel witnessing this love he had for this child. I had no idea my dad was capable of this kind of love because he had never shown it to me.

Being vulnerable and looking for love any way that I could get it, I became sexually active at a young age. I thought sex with a person meant that person loved me. I thought this way because no one ever told me any better, and the guys would tell me whatever I needed to hear just to get what they wanted. Although I was older, on the inside I was still that same little girl longing for affection and love from her dad.

The first time I had sex, I felt terrible afterwards. I immediately regretted my decision and wished I had waited. I was pressured into doing something that I wasn't ready for with a man who wanted a virgin. I was left with an empty feeling while this man's ego had been stroked. I remember walking home in pain and crying on the inside, because I knew it was something I could never take back. I had no one to talk to about this because I should have known better, I thought. I let him groom me into a fool, and it all went downhill from there. But was it really this man who took my virginity that groomed me into a fool or was it my dad that did the grooming?

I've been working on and building my relationship with God. In order to do that, I've learned to come to terms with the decisions I have made and the consequences along with them. True, my dad did not help the situation at all; he should have been someone who should have protected me and prepared me for what was in store. Still, I take responsibility for my actions and the result of them. Now that I know better, I try to do better.

So, I Just RIDE!!!

I drive fast. I am alone at midnight. I have been trying hard not to get into trouble, but I have a war in my mind, I just ride!!!! The highway is therapeutic - always has been. Looking back, my dad used to just get up and get on the highway and just ride (as he would tell me); that's the way my father made his life an art form.

I'm tired of feeling like I'm fucking crazy. I'm tired of driving until I see stars in my eyes. This is all I've got to keep myself sane. So, I just RIDE!!!

I AM – A DAUGHTER OF A QUEEN
(UNKNOWINGLY)

Mom,

That man chose not to be the head. I couldn't fathom how much hurt you'd endured throughout your life, that you had to push to the side and never got to heal from but only in the way that you knew; the hurt you've encountered from men, having to suck it up and keep pressing forward; the five children to raise alone with faith knowing God is the father to the fatherless. You didn't show a lot of physical emotions toward us.

Love wasn't affectionate. I don't recall you really hugging us or saying you love us, but through every action, we knew how much you loved and cared for us. Love showed through your actions: Cooking, cleaning, providing us a stable home, introducing us to God. You cared for us with every breath in you. You didn't play with us and over us. You did what you could do!

Mom, you have been such a tremendous asset in my life. You are the force that binds the pieces of life together. Life is so beautiful because I have a mother like you who was and is always there for me. I've only seen you cry out of frustration, but I've never seen you depend on anyone but God! I thank you for being God-fearing and putting God as a head of our household. Your faith and belief in God have instilled in me the desire to work on my relationship with Him.

As I got older, I realized that my dad didn't really help you financially with me, as far as buying clothes and shoes, for instance. I remember when I got older that you gave me a Social Security check for $33 a month. You said that you felt like I was old enough to get some money so I could start buying some things for myself. At that age I didn't really know that $33 wasn't a lot of money. I remember when I used to ask my dad for money, and he would say your mom gets a check for you and that I must be spending it. It was $33 – what else would he expect her to do with it? Start me a college fund? I may have wished you could have had more money or ways to keep us more active, but I thank God for what you could do. Even with that $33 a month, it was the beginning of something for me.

One day I picked up some hair with my money, and the rest is history. I started practicing braiding on my nieces' hair, and then I started doing my friends' hair. I even started doing the hair of the kids in the community before I started branching out to my friends in school. Ronnie, my sister, said she always believed in me, and she pushed me no matter what. We would even go out of town together and make some money with my braiding, which I was proud to show my mom. Once I did share this with my mom, and she knew I had the potential to make money, she pretty much left it in my hands to take care of myself. I was okay with that though. She really didn't have the means to keep taking care of me now that

I was older, but she didn't leave me in a situation to be by myself either. This whole situation taught me to hustle, so I kept my pocket full of money, and I worked for it.

I always knew that I could count on you, mom. When I looked into the crowd at a talent show or graduation, you always sat in the crowd. While I could always count on you being present, my dad was never present. Like, what the fuck was he doing to never be around? Like, damn! Was he that caught up in a woman that he'd just fuck me and my siblings around? Must be nice, I guess.

Mom, I'm a lot like you in many ways. I AM you in so many ways. I don't even think you have taken the time to realize that. I've totally replayed your life over in lots of situations not knowing this stuff carried over to me. I sit sometimes and hear myself sounding like you, and I even run home like you. I've witnessed you work hard every day of my life, with no complaints. I watched you get prepared to go provide for us daily. I never knew if you were tired, although looking back on it now, I'm sure you were. But you never complained. You got up every morning, took your bath, and prepared for your day.

I have never seen a woman as strong as you. Having to care for five children the best way you could. Growing up I didn't know we were poor or if we lacked anything because you made it seem and feel like we were living a good life. We never missed a meal and we always dressed nice. You are the most beautiful piece of art I've ever seen in my life. Strong and courageous you are. Strong minded and determined. You could have chosen to do anything with your life, but you chose to take responsibility and care for us regardless of what dreams you had for your life or preferred to be doing.

You've been hurt so much but still found a way to figure out how to love us. You held us accountable so that we could be prepared for what was to come in this cruel world. I thank you for teaching me to become responsible enough to pay bills and carry out tasks as simple as going to the neighbor's house to relay a message. As much as I complained as a child, I appreciate sweeping the neighborhood streets and parking lots. It taught me how to appreciate any place of residence that I would occupy. I appreciate you taking us to church Wednesdays and Saturdays. I didn't get to experience traffic throughout our home, parties, or the drug house. Everything I've learned about that life was outside of our home.

You didn't share a lot of things with me. It's like the older I got God put it on me to push it out of you. I wish you were able to experience life and live to the fullest. I wish your grandparents who raised you taught you love. I wish our fathers would have taken responsibility for us so that you wouldn't have had to work yourself into the ground. I wish you would have had the resources to keep active in sports and taking trips. I love you for doing what you had to do and making use of what you had.

Mom, I wanna see you happy and smiling more. The abuse and toxic relationships made you feel like nothing, along with your own sisters being horrible to you. But all and all, you thanked God for everything. I wouldn't ask God for a better Mother!

There are some things that affected me throughout my life.
Why did you place your fear in me selfishly? You are the most hidden treasure that I wish could be found. You are rare! Everything that was meant to break you, you overcame. I see the pain in your eyes as you wonder when my turn will come. Mom, I am the daughter of a Queen. I am your Queen. I am You!

I AM - UNTAUGHT

"Just go to school, come home, and do your chores" - that's what I was told. I was always able to go outside and play with friends, but those streetlights had better not come on before I made it back home. I was able to be outside the community with friends, riding bikes, playing at the playgrounds, hanging at the local schools, and walking to different corner stores. I was never able to spend the night with friends though, especially if it was a man in the home. I never understood why. I would ask until I had tears in my eyes begging to stay with my friends, but my mother wouldn't let up. She was firm! Her "no" meant no!

C hildhood, to me, appeared to be easy. I had no worries or no responsibilities. The only exceptions were probably church and school – attending those places was expected of me. We attended church every Saturday - Adventist Youth - in the evenings and prayer meetings on weekdays. I loved going to church. I loved our church family, and the friendships we made would last a lifetime.

Then there were the errands we had to manage without a vehicle. When it came to doing laundry, we used to take the cab to the laundromat. Although they were chores, I enjoyed those times because they were like taking vacations away from our neighborhood. I remember always looking out the window of the cab, looking into the sky and smiling as we drove off. I was excited anticipating playing in the arcade and using the coins to purchase candy and pop. My mother made it look easy, and we were never out of line or asked questions that did not pertain to being a child. I knew my mother was a hard worker. She was always tired, so I wasn't always able to do a lot of things that the other kids my age around my neighborhood could do. That was a good thing though, as she was looking out for my well-being. My mother did her best with the time and resources she had, but I was still lacking to a certain degree.

As I sit, I think of all these people surrounding me that have my best interests at heart. My protectors, my advocates. Back then, looking over my life, I did not have a lot of that protection. I WAS UNTAUGHT! I wasn't taught anything that would help me get through life. I wasn't taught what to look out for, what type of guys not to encounter. I wasn't taught how a man is supposed to treat a woman. I wasn't taught how to fight. I had no one to talk to me about peer-pressure. I didn't have those talks with anyone about sex. I didn't have anyone with whom to share my secrets. Or anyone to share a special handshake. I didn't take special trips with anyone. I didn't get to feel that connection that I saw a lot of young siblings have with their older siblings or parents. Even missing all of that, I was still molded but not in a positive way. My father never taught me anything to remember but "fuck a nigga!" and "you don't need a nigga!"

Mom, your life consisted of work. You did what you could. But what could any of you teach me that you were never taught? I don't blame you, it's not your fault. All of us have had to grow into situations we weren't ready for. I learned from every situation I encountered - good or bad. If I only knew that all of this that I lacked would surface in my life and play a major role in my life more than I anticipated.

How did this happen?
How did I become the one everyone forgot about?

I AM – THE BABY SISTER

*Little, but big, brother, you made it known I was a mistake daily.
"Mom found you in the dumpster. She felt so sorry for you, so she
brought you home," you'd say then laugh. I died on the inside.*

*I was a joke to you. Everything about me was a joke to you. You
really knew how to bring out the stupid in me. You made fun of me about
everything. We created a relationship out of bullying. I wanted to do
everything right so I wouldn't be the butt of your jokes anymore. Wishful
thinking! We never sat and talked about anything serious, nor could I
trust you with any information. Why was I so funny to you? I wondered.
You made me feel like I wasn't ever going to be loved by anyone. You
embarrassed me about things that should have been between us both,
being my big brother and all. Why did you treat me like shit?*

*Was I paying for mom's mistake in your eyes?
Why was I a target for you to torture?*

I remember you sat and threw a football at my chest for hours and made me take it. That hurt so much. You laughed at me all the time when my dad would disappoint me or buy me something only to take it back.

Why did me grabbing your shirt make you knock my teeth out? I remember I asked my dad for $20, and he said he didn't have it. But when you turned around and asked him for it, he gave you $120! You laughed so hard in my face. What you showed me was that my dad would rather do it for another kid, just not his. All those times you clowned me for pissing the bed and telling everyone about it. You could've helped me. I did have a problem. I wanted to confide in you. I love you so much; you're my big brother. I needed you way more than you know, but you never made yourself available in that aspect. My kids needed you. They have absent fathers, but you created your own family that you cherish with all your heart. No need for us anymore.

Being the baby girl out of five, I spent a lot of time with my older sisters. Little sisters are responsible for keeping you from doing a lot of regrettable things, simply by the fact that most little sisters look up to their big sisters. Being the youngest of all my siblings – my sisters and brothers - comes with its own set of privileges. We are the most pampered kid of the family that can get away with anything and everything. The elder siblings are always there to protect you.

I watched my older siblings living their lives with their children, going to school, and doing extracurricular activities. My brother was always able to do whatever he wanted - coming and going, living his life, and partying as he pleased. He always laughed at me and in my face growing up. Anything I couldn't do or would get in trouble for was always funny to him. It upset me a lot. Witnessing my brother coming home drunk and then watching my mom deal with his behavior was my first exposure to alcoholism, and I hated it. Then fast forward, I would end up dealing with two boyfriends that abused alcohol and women.

With my eldest brother, I always wanted to tag along with him, but he was always busy. I always watched him come and go. Watching him cut hair was the only time I was able to be around him for long periods of time. I would pull up a chair and just sit and watch him do what he loved. I would laugh at the conversations the fellas were having, and I admired the attention I got from being his cute little sister. Seeing him smile warmed my heart. It made me feel wanted in his world. I would cry because I wanted to be with him, but he would always say, "You can't go with me, baby. I'll be back, okay?"

With my head hanging low, I'd reply, "Okay."

Watching him leave mom's house with his buddies and smiling, I wished it was me leaving with him instead. I never experienced the talks that a big brother would give his baby sister. I built a life-long relationship sitting with my him because that was my time I could have with him. Otherwise, I was watching him come home intoxicated and hearing my mom yell because he was so intoxicated. He didn't know what he was doing. Then I found myself getting involved with an alcoholic, and my God! I wouldn't wish that type an alcoholic person on anyone. I never saw healthy relationships, healthy boundaries, or healthy situations within anyone's situation.

As a child, I witnessed a lot of hurt and abuse in my eldest sister. How could someone so beautiful, smart, outgoing, bright, harmless, loving, caring, self-less, and ambitious - a queen - be treated like this? I mean, she would give you the world. When I was younger, we never had in-depth talks of what to do or what not to do. I built a strong bond with her, never wanting to leave her to be hurt. We were each other's safe haven. I love her so much and hold her so close to my heart. The bond isn't your original sister relationship. It's more so mom-daughter. My best friend in a sense, my sister gave me some of the purest love I'd never received from anyone. I believe the feeling is mutual on her end as well. This supernatural bond we share is indescribable.

I remember when I had my first kid. The experience my sister and I shared together was like none other. Each contraction was a spark. My final push bringing him into this world, I remember she threw up. My sister conceived my child with me. That's only something God can do. I always wanted to live with my sister and further my education with her guidance, but my mom wouldn't ever consider it. My sister always spoke life into me. She fought to push me to be the best version of me, the version that I didn't see in myself. I knew I was something special in her eyes. She still gives me this look as if Mom is just bringing me home from the hospital. She's my ROCK! I sit and watch her like a little kid smiling as I see her glowing, finding her purpose in life, and creating paths. I admire the way she supports my nieces in any way that she can. Only if I had that support - the things I would've accomplished.

The third oldest sister, I felt she hated me because somehow, she was more responsible for me than anyone else. Daily, she would make sure my hair was combed, prepared my meals, and prepped my clothes for school. She would wake me up every morning and fuss about me pushing her behind on getting her own self ready to start the day. She taught me how to sit properly at a table, taught me the names of the utensils we used to eat with, how to sell candy, and how to make money. She wanted to go and enjoy your life, but she had to take me along with her. We built a relationship of survival amongst our situation. I enjoyed every moment she despised having to bring me along.

I remember our conversations vividly. She talked to me the most about the importance of things. She gave me advice that would help me carry out different situations throughout my life. She always stopped me in my tracks to try to get to know me, to know how I felt about situations, and at least know some of the things I was going through. She taught me how to do things with my kids. She also helped me accept my first child and to understand the underlying hurt and the recognition of why I chose the type of boys I dealt with. I love her for that. She wouldn't understand how much the little things she did meant to me. I watched her go through relationship struggles, but she had a different way of showing hurt and letting anybody in her space. She happens to be my greatest mystery. She always makes me think. She may not understand, but I'm the only one who breaks the code every time. I can see her smile as I type, "How you know?" with those Chiclet teeth (as I always say when she smiles). I did a lot of first things with her. I'll always cherish it. We can sit and literally talk about anything after we talk trash first. Then she'll say, "Nawl, but seriously…" then it's on. Sister, I miss you; I miss us; I miss "we."

Everybody molded my life and went on about their own lives, even when I acted as babysitter to their kids. Still, I was left to deal with a lot of things I should've been able to come to my siblings about. I was left hurting, expecting understanding, but all I got was blamed. My big brothers didn't fight for me. I had to fight alone. I had been fighting all my life to secure spots in their lives. I wasn't told what to look out for. I always heard, "I think she was letting him take advantage of her," while they laughed.

I was always told I was just like my daddy. I was told a brother is the next best thing to a father when it comes to your kids. I didn't get to experience that. My kids were pushed to the side like everything else. From my brothers and sisters, I was left with the same feeling my dad left me with - the feeling of being alone.

Lord! What did I do for my kids to be abandoned as well?
The public figures, community leaders, and kid advocates forgot

about my kids, their own flesh and blood. I was hurting so bad and down to nothing lots of the time, but I saw help being offered to strangers instead. I've cried so much over the years in my life but never showed it. I always had to wear a smile. Absolutely nobody wanted to hear me vent about anything. I've held onto the pain. I just needed someone to listen to, but it made me depend on God. I've made it a habit to run to God about anything. No matter where I'm at.

They forgot about me!

I AM – YOUR MOTHER, UNPLANNED

How worthless are you? You're pathetic! You ought to be ashamed of yourself! You can't even find nobody that loves you. Your own fucking kids are not even listening to you (shaking my head). Your mother and your father didn't teach you anything. You don't even know how to choose the right person. All you do is attract people that want something from you and could care less about you. You said every day you're capable. You're not even worthy enough for anybody that wants to be in your life nor want to be in your kids' life. You're stuck with children and their fathers don't even want to be present.

Girl, what the fuck did you do?

Why didn't you have an abortion when you got pregnant? You could've been living your life without any responsibilities, but you were listening to your mother saying she don't believe in abortions. Look at

how it cost you. You can't get a nanny or your family to help you. You can't even get anybody to watch the kids while you go to work - that's a damn shame. Yeah, your own brothers and sisters treat your ass like you are invisible until they need something from you; then you are beneficial. Suck that shit up - that's all you know. Anyway, suck it up and deal with people's shit. Why the fuck you keep crying? Ain't nobody gonna help you. Your own father sits and watches you struggle and still doesn't feel the need to help you or be involved in your life because those are your kids. He didn't fuck you to make these kids.
He's living his life. He reminds you of that every time you need help.

Sonshine! That is what I call you, my firstborn son. Crazy how things turn out. The child whom you were left alone with to care for. Meanwhile, being an innocent but lonely, lost, confused, bright, loving, daydreaming, no potential young girl, I wasn't sure on how to raise you. Meanwhile, I didn't want to raise you. Neither did the man who groomed me into placing you in me. Where did the hate for me come from? Did the love for your absent father with no moral support in no form enrage you? Furious I am. Hurt I am. Lost as I am, God, I place my son, our situations, and his dad in your hands. I have no control, and honestly, I don't want control. I'm tired. I fought a fight you would never know about or understand. Your father will never be a man to teach and tell you. Years of hurt, lies, physical and mental abuse, manipulation, betrayal, and more years of control and hurt with you and over you.

You're growing into this young unknown man. I can't fight with you. I'm exhausted. You wouldn't care or understand. So, I have to fight with the word of God and pray because the devil has set in and seems to navigate your actions. No matter how you may feel, I still will not tolerate your disrespect. You will not disrespect my home. In my home, you will work and continue your education. You will interact with your siblings and show love and compassion. You will respect me as your mother and talk to me with respect. To think you got up one day in my face and called me "bruh" and said what you would do to me. I no longer have anything to say or do with you. Until you realize where you went wrong and apologize, I guess that's it for us, son. How your father makes you feel comfortable in disrespecting me and not making it right is beyond me. But he's a foolish, disrespectful person. Good luck to the both of you.

Lord, I ask that I don't become a grandparent in the process of all this. But it's out of my hands literally. It hurts knowing I have sacrificed my whole life for you to then have you treat me like you do and feel the way you feel about me. I wish nothing but the best for you. I pray for you and pray God to guide you throughout your life. I pray you do the things that I have taught you. I pray you use your head in your decision making and take care of your business. But no matter what, I love you, and you will always be my baby.

Your dad said that I fucked your life up, but he ain't never had to be responsible. What is he doing any different than I did now that you're staying with him? He's your dad but he is still not acting and fathering responsibly. He didn't even show up for the birth of his first son, the one that he tells the world that he loves so much. But I fucked your life up? Stupid! But what did I think? And my second son's dad is right down the street and won't even come say hi to him, come get him, or spend any time with him.

The dad of my twins intentionally fucked my life up – he fucking beat my ass and tried to finish driving me to kill myself, knowing that my other kids' dads did the same to me. I looked past a lot of things based off seeing potential in him. But there was a lot of verbal abuse and antagonizing. When I moved back home for a surgery, I ended up moving in with him and felt trapped and controlled. There was so much disrespect. Did I think that he wasn't gonna do my stupid fat ass the same way?

As they all say to me: With yo' stupid fat gullible ass - don't nobody want you. They just wanna fuck and use my stupid ass. Am I not worthy of nothing good? Look at you - you got four kids and three absentee dads. You're doing everything on your own. They only call you and stress you. They say, "Fuck those kids," and their families won't help either. You can't even work a job; you're tired, stressed, depressed, and wanna give up. You regret all of your kids; you're stuck and can't move on. Your kids are hardheaded and don't listen. And the only advice anybody got for you is, "Those are your kids! You should've made better choices. You picked the niggas to have kids by. I don't know what to tell you - figure it out. You sure chose a bunch of sad niggas to have some kids by. How are you gonna get mad?"

I had four kids and their daddies left me, but then to have my own son to get older and do the same! I remember that my oldest son's father told me that our son would beat my ass one day, and sure enough my son did try to run up on me – his mother. I was the one person who gave my all for him and tried to raise him into a man. He had to leave my house after that. He lives with his father, who isn't a good example and steady talks shit about me to him; what grown-ass man talks shit to his son about the woman that gave him life? His father just lets him sit around and do anything at his house. My son barely graduated, but he did. It hurt my heart, but I could not bring myself to attend his graduation. Did he want me there? Was he sad about my absence? I can't say for sure. My son and I have some healing and mending to do, but until he learns how to respect me and his siblings, I must love him from afar. My son has to learn on his own in the meantime.

Am I the problem! I'm sick of this shit! All these dudes have degraded me, beat my ass, dragged my name through the dirt, cheated on me, disrespected me in front of strangers, broke my face, almost broke my throat and neck, beat my ass in front of my kids, and called me out my name in front of them. I still have the scars today-physically (even if you can't see them, I can) and mentally. All I know is abuse! By men who could not even get off their own moms' titties as grown ass men.

I've never experienced love in its full form. I don't think I ever will. You've been dealt a bad hand, honey, all your life, Nakia. What have you done? Where do I get this shit from? Why am I not capable of love? I watch people find love. I watch people date, get engaged, and all types of stuff, but I have yet to experience that. All I do is give love but ain't gonna ever get it back. Then I have the audacity to save these little boys after almost costing me my life. I even try to be considerate of these little boys, still try to co-parent with these little boys, still keep an open door that they have already chosen not to walk in. I have to be by far the dumbest person I've encountered.

Parasites live off of you and gravitate to the source to drain every bit out of you until you are no more. I've had my fair share of fixer uppers; that's all I knew. I kept placing the wrong people in my space, turning my right place into the wrong one. Displaced people will really have us second guessing ourselves. They will really have us out here thinking that we are asking for too much. The truth is they can't offer us anything. I was seeking validation from someone who's not even valid for my destination in my life. We have been wired to help. We risk confusing your contribution as confirmation thinking we've found someone, and that's not what God wanted for us. That's why it's important to know our value when helping because we choose to date "projects". Don't feel bad about cutting the string when God handed us the scissors, so that we won't take on responsibilities that only should come when we are placed in the role of "wife," and he is in the role of your "husband." Don't date projects! Never feel bad for walking away. Keep boundaries in place. You simply just help. I was just tired. I was burned out trying to give from a place of nothing. The tank of loving myself was empty. I had to get myself in order. I couldn't love if I didn't love myself. I couldn't be happy. Rejection hit me so hard because I had rejected me before they would reject me.

Manipulation is physiological abuse to its core. It sells dreams and nightmares. It will have you working hard for what you really don't want. It needs control. The men I dealt with were so insecure that they twisted their flaws and made them my flaws because they were damaged. They were so insecure because they knew I was settling to be with them. We will always experience a migraine in our souls when you allow someone else's thoughts to align what you think about you.

I was always put on hold or given some bullshit excuse as to why I was put on hold. And everybody wanted me to sit around and wait! For real, God?! This is what this is, huh? I realized I got so accustomed to average that my whole frustration in my life was about bills and what I wanted. I sat alone and cried and screamed in my living room, telling God I knew this was not what He had for me; to pay bills, to parent alone, be stressed, depressed, frustrated, and regretting my children. And then die? Lord! I know it was God who led me to them and placed them in my life, but what's my purpose? I'm tired of doing things my way. It ain't working my way. I'm tired!! I can't bear anymore burdens alone that people have left with me. I'm all yours. Lead me. I'm listening. Thank you, Lord!

I AM – A SURVIVOR

Excited! Words cannot express how I was feeling that day, backtracking on how I had a feeling all month that something wasn't right. But willing to look past shit as always. I got a notification informing me that the guy I opened up and had given in to had been dealing with someone else. Boom! Typical shit as soon as I said okay. And I let my guard down. This happens only for me to say to myself, "Bitch, you still don't know your worth? How do you know what love is? How? Nakia, how are you still unsure of what you deserve?! I'm angry at myself; angry that I don't speak up enough for myself, angry that I don't demand enough; angry that I don't walk away when I should, knowing that this is going to break me down, wondering and thinking of what's going on; angry because I'm working hard, trying to prove and show respect and be respectful. I get FUCKED as usual! Wondering how someone can look at you, demand, and make you feel like what you're doing is wrong. Meanwhile, they're wrong! I'm broken - not fully but partially. I'm proud. I know there's some growth. I was so hurt but had to show face to my kids. I know for sure this is not going to be the end of the disappointments, but I must talk to God to see what is it that I should do regarding the situation. I love him but I also must love me even more. I feel like I'm placed here to give love but not be loved!

Signed,

Lonely Heart!

T his just might be the hardest thing I ever had to do. I never thought I'd see the day I'd be living without you. I realized all the promises you made to me through the years and all the times I forgave you even when you caused me tears. But I just can't do it - I can't let you do it again. At age 35, I realized that I was a survivor.

I couldn't distinguish you between anything. I had no boundaries with you at all. I allowed you to come in and take over everything I had in me and outside of me. I chose you over everything that wanted me from the heart. Your words sounded better than a love song from the 90s. There wasn't anything better than 90s music. All I've ever seen throughout my childhood was you. You were close to being blood; couldn't make us any more kin. You have lived with us all my life as far as I can remember. You even moved out with me when I got grown - at least I felt grown. Sometimes you'll still stop by and say hello from time to time. I loved you so much, I accepted you at all costs, but it cost me everything in my life: my mental, my emotional, my physical, and spiritual. I know you're probably reading this saying, "This ain't happening."

You had my best interest, at least I thought. You knew about me in ways a lot of people didn't know about me, but instead of comforting me and being there, you took advantage of me. You molded me and made me feel like you cared. I was naive and couldn't distinguish the two. You made me acceptive of lying to make you feel good. you pressured me out of something that was so precious in God's eyes; you pressured me out of something I never thought to give away. I was your project. I was something you preyed on, and you were a liar, but the lies caused you something you never got back. The seal was broken. As I sit with pain and regret, as you smile of a well-deserved accomplishment, you didn't deserve any part of me. You caused me hurt that would lead me into more destruction. But I'm done blaming you - I blame myself now. I allowed you. I didn't know myself. I didn't know the gift God had in me. I was lost and looking for love that I lacked.

Recently I sat and watched segments of a speaker discussing the topics of God, sex, and getting out of unwanted situations that God does not require of you. I spent all this time working on myself, only to realize again that I'm still fucked up! I still allowed the same spirit and behavior with a different face to enter my life and put me back in the same place. He was aggressive, ignorant, lacking knowledge, stuck, resistant to change, and abusive.

I recall one morning getting dressed and simply asking him what time he planned to get up and speak with a guy at his job, and he got so angry and aggressive with me. He accused me of talking to him like he was a kid. I was confused and angry. As I questioned him about his reaction and disrespect to me, my kids, and my family, he proceeded to punch me in my face. My fucking face!! Really? Then he began to put me down, calling me lame and telling me that nobody wanted me or my kids.

"Ain't nobody gonna deal with y'all. You a hoe! Don't nobody wanna be with you. They just wanna fuck you." These were the same words from my previous relationships. I was numb. Because I damn near felt like this.

Unworthy! My own father never made me feel unworthy - just worthless. I was unworthy of my children's fathers wanting to take care of them. Unworthy of my father wanting to show me the way. Unworthy of getting help from a village that's supposed to be there. Unworthy of opportunities that are available but never given or offered to me. Unworthy of being able to express myself. Unworthy of people giving me the same love and respect that I give to them. I'm just fucking worthless!

I believed that men had a right to me. I became more obese, wearing t-shirts and oversized, male-styled clothing so that men wouldn't find me attractive. My weight became my protection from the unwanted advances of men. But that still didn't work. I was comfortable in codependency. I was afraid of life. I was afraid to be alone. I loved the way men lied. Unknowingly!

Something was wrong with me. I had not learned yet. I was still not able to tell the difference between a man versus a boy, and I dealt with boys. In my relationships with my kids' fathers, I experienced all kinds of abuse – even physically during my pregnancy – trauma, cheating, and losing myself trying to be what they wanted me to be as a woman or trying to be, in a sense, their mother.

What's wrong with me? Why am I always a punching bag? Why am I always the go-to? Why am I never thought of? Why am I always giving? Why am I always suffering? Why do I have to put up with shit all the time? Why me? Then the fight always came in when these men knew that I did not need them and stopped being co-dependent on them. They did not like that, as they were still trying to figure themselves out. I always stood up for myself, but I also lost myself often. God didn't create me to fit in at all.

What was I losing anyway, besides dick? I finally made the decision to go celibate, cold turkey. I tested myself by seeing how accessible I would make myself as the people in my life reached out. I had to learn to make my "no" mean "no!" This is the stage in my life, right now, where I'm putting on my big girl panties. There are not enough of these that can satisfy me - "I love you" or "You're so pretty." I'm being completely transparent when I say this, but needy people are the absolute worst people to be around. They are like a strainer, and no matter how much you fill it up, it will never be enough for the needy person. Whatever love you put in them will seep out.

I thank God with all my heart that he kept me, because all I was doing was being drained of everything within me. I was left lifeless time and time again. I've been at the bottom to the point where I didn't even see that I had no life in me. When your heart is pure, you do things out of the kindness of your heart. The devil moves right in to kill, steal, and destroy "YOU," and leave you for dead. Because of God's grace and his mercy, He sends His angels to save you every time, because He knows where He needs you to be despite any situation that was meant to kill you.

Now that I'm in the healing process of my life and walking into purpose. I realized I've been running from God unknowingly. I believe God is calling me to be a prophet. I love being alone but never utilize my time. Allowing myself to become distracted by people, places and different things. I am a survivor of domestic violence. I had several relationships/situation-ships that involved physical, mental and emotional abuse. I realized when we don't believe we are good enough, we continue to hang around others that reinforce these feelings. I found myself attracted to men who were rude and didn't care about my feelings. I always despised my kind nature and my concern for others. I cared too much about people and their feelings. I admired people who could say what they meant and didn't care how others responded. Whenever I would treat people how they treated me, I was a horrible person. I recognized this was a form of manipulation. It wasn't until I learned a valuable lesson. You should always be your authentic self.

The situations were the same just with a different face each time. I realized some people hate themselves and they don't have the ability to accept love. Love feels foreign to them, so they reject the people that love them. Everybody wanted to take everything from me but gave nothing. I knew what I brought to the table and what I was capable of. What I didn't have was self-worth. I didn't know how to determine the capacity of the person you interact with and know what to require of a man or how much love, truth, appreciation and honesty they can handle. I had to learn to watch the people I chose to connect with because some people don't have your best interest at heart. I cried so hard one day asking God to show me where I went wrong dealing with these relationships with family and friends. I wasn't wary of people who were cool with my weaknesses and comfortable with me being stuck with stagnation and lack of mobility.

So many people I know, they just want to touch me! I'm wondering what's my purpose on this planet Earth, wondering will I ever find true love. Will I have a husband? Someone that admires me in the same exact manner that I love them? Why do I feel so alone? I'm surrounded by many people but so alone. Always waiting for someone to walk out. Leaving without notice. Causing disappointment in any way possible. All I do is sit and accept circumstances that come my way. I'm subject to hurt; it's all I know. Crazy, huh? A broken mother's and lost father's scorned child searching for God to show me signs, answers and ways to heal.

I look into my eyes and say to myself:

Nakia, you, baby girl, are beautiful, but you don't know it. You are smart. You are loved but don't receive it. You have a beautiful smile. You have an amazing personality, but it's all about the things that look good.

Nakia, let's be honest: you are hurt, you are ashamed, abused, disrespected, left behind, not cherished, used, sad, hurt by the ones you love, looked past, won't find closure or love, single, single-parent, bastard, useless, hopeless, will never make it, failure. You will always be good enough for someone to use or need in their time. Your children don't love you, yet you're stuck caring for them. Your children's dads don't respect you and won't offer you help.'

What did I do to deserve this torture? I wouldn't wish any mom having to do and deal with the things I deal with. It hurts. I'm not scared to say it anymore. Not at all!

I AM – NOT LIKE EVERYBODY ELSE

Depression wants to darken my days. End my life. Keep me from interacting and wanting to deal with my kids. Anxiety wants me to go crazy. Overthink every situation that would benefit me long-term. Battling this daily is a fight that you can't win without God. There are many sleepless nights. No sleep until my body literally gives out on me. Depression that causes me to overreact consistently. I hate it! Trauma from abuse and things that have gone on in my life has caused so much damage. Why me? But why not me?! A life struggle while raising four kids on top of it. Lord, I know you are in the midst, and I know you have to allow me to understand and learn from mistakes as well.

I am not like everybody else. I don't mind telling you how I went to counseling and how it helped me. Or how I went to the doctor after contracting STDs several times. My doctor sat me down and talked to me as if I were her child because it hurt her so bad to see that I was coming in here to get cured repeatedly. She finally said to me, "Nakia do you know who you are?"

She also asked me if I loved myself. She asked because if I loved myself, why did I not love myself enough to stop these visits to keep being told that I had another STD. My doctor said she saw greatness and something better for me. She then looked me in my eyes and said, "Honey, leave that no good guy alone. He's killing your body, and it is clear that he doesn't have no respect, nor do he care about you enough to put a condom on, yet alone stop cheating."

I was so young and lost, extra hurt, and full of rage, only to find out that he – this no-good guy – was her patient and was coming to get cured, not tell even telling me shit. How could I just accept that? I was so naïve. I didn't even confront him; not one time. I just dealt with it and kept scarfing down pills as if I was totally fine.

All my life I've been told to shut up or told I don't know what I'm talking about. I've questioned myself about why I always disregarded and looked over for everything? This may go on all my whole life. Nobody ever asked me how I felt about anything. I've always just dealt with everything no matter what it was. This included being pregnant at an early age and not having a say on whether I would like to keep the child, give it up for adoption, or have an abortion. I had to go off someone else's belief about what was best for me but never my own belief. Even in relationships, the guy just cheated and do whatever they wanted but nobody ever asked me was I okay.

When I spoke up and said something, I was the problem. Every time I spoke up for myself or said no, I was the problem; I was angry; I was this; I was that. It was always "you're gonna do what I tell you to do." It took me getting to the age of 34 to realize how much I did not control my own life, and once I stood up for myself, I got disconnected from just about everybody I dealt with. I thought it was a bad thing. I was even scared to be disconnected from everyone, but once I realized that was the best thing for me, I felt so much better. Even when they would say that I think I'm better than everybody, I'd laugh on the inside because in my mind I'd think that I still ain't got shit, but y'all mad and treating me like I'm better than.

I've been crossed by people I'd give the shirt off my back and the shoes off my feet - family, friends and associates.

My heart is so big, and the ones who know play on that. The ones who don't know miss out on it. I just wanna love and save everyone, but whose gonna save me after it's all said and done? Trusting God and his Word, I know He's the only one who can and will save me. I am thankful for the unexpected help God has given me when I couldn't see a way out. I still have a way to go; I'm a work in progress.

In the meantime, He sends the right people in my life to help me, like my doctor. She offered me help, and I took it! I went through four consultations before I connected with one consistently. Seeking help was the best thing I could have ever done. They have helped me through several stages of my life. When I feel that we have ran out our course, I'll seek more professional help. Having someone to talk to that won't judge me or throw my past in my face but help me face the problem and fight through it with me. I am not HEALED. I'm simply HEALING.

Healing doesn't have a time limit. It's a journey from God so you can reach your potential. You will get discouraged, depressed, sidetracked and more. It's not easy but it's totally worth it.

I AM – AN ENTREPRENEUR

*I have no support! But I decided that I would never be anyone's victim
again.*

Initially, having no support was disappointing, as it felt like no one was
supportive of my entrepreneurial endeavors. I have power because I
have power of choice. I felt stuck at my jobs, so I stopped limiting my
beliefs and started working for myself. Singapore is a place where most
people know at least one to two people working on building a business
or already have one established, so it was hard to imagine that almost
everyone I approached didn't know any entrepreneurs. As for those who
said that they would help but never did (even after I followed up), it felt like
they were paying lip service.

However, when I reflected on the situation, I realized that they were not being unsupportive, but merely offering what they could in their capacity. Some may not be willing to go the extra mile to do such a favor for someone unless it is very close kin. Others may not be in close contact with their business friends. Hence, it would have been too much of a hassle to reach out to them for an offbeat request like this. As for the people who promised to reach out but never did, perhaps they wanted to reject my request for the same reason but felt awkward doing so because they didn't know how to say no.

Instead of faulting them for being unsupportive, I should be more appreciative of the handful of gems who pushed through with the favor in the end. And I am definitely appreciative after coming to this realization. These are the people whom I know I can't rely on for any further help in the future, and also the people I'd go out of my way to help in the future (not to say that I wouldn't help those who didn't help me, but that I would make more of an effort to help the people who have supported me).

I had to recognize that it is not reasonable to expect full support from your friends and family all the time, for every single goal you pursue. I read articles on what not to expect when starting my own business and things to look out for. It was a hard pill to swallow but the cure to stop feeling the way I felt. It helped me determine who should be allowed and not allowed in my life. People will band together against you to prevent you from reaching your purpose. I liked the affirmations and attention that comes with broadcasting your plans, but I had to learn how to move in silence because everyone that smiles in your face is not happy about your growth and your dreams. I have to prevent oversharing until I'm in a position of manifestation and I have finished my project.

I am the CEO of my life and I have the power to shift and align my squad. Remember, girls have a lot of friends. Women have a handful or few, while queens stand alone and never have one or more friends. Others are business partners, associates, employees, or people that she knows. My hard work will speak for itself without the sabotage of others. It has taught me to protect my heart and dreams. When they ask me who I am, I will be able to say. I Am Nakia... CEO, Author, Motivational Speaker, and more.

I AM – CHOOSING ME, UNAPOLOGETICALLY

Choosing ME has been the hardest thing I've ever done in my entire life. I've always picked everyone over myself. I chose to choose me, and it has cost me friendships, relationships I've never thought would clash. I chose to allow God to show me the things that I was blind to over the years. In my thoughts, muthafuckas really have been using me for their greater good. As much as it hurts, it feels so good. The burden is being lifted. The light is shining at the end of the tunnel. God has sent three people to me with the same message. Crazy right? But I'm shifting and not asking any questions because God has seen and heard my cries for years. I don't wanna be bitter anymore. I don't wanna hate or hurt anymore. I choose not to allow myself to get on the level of anyone who treats me like crap.

Healing and restoration are what I'm seeking in my life at this moment. I want to heal and right my wrongs – those that were done knowingly and unknowingly. I want God to keep my child safe – bring him home in due time – but I want to be ready to accept anything my child may feel I could've been better at or things I could've done.

On the flip side, I've done what I knew to do and what was left for me to do. I shouldn't have had to play both roles. I wasn't able to let my son see the side of me he should have been able to see. I don't want to keep emotionally disregarding my children because of my own issues. It's hard!

I don't want to keep being mad because I'm a parent and I must take care of these children by myself. My children deserve to see me happy and deserve to get a better and healthier version of me. My children won't be sitting in someone else's chair trying to find a way to cope, how to find love, and figure out life outside of my mishaps. Turning pain into power!

I intend to learn and grow until the moment that I breathe my last breath. I am truly excited at the growth that I have experienced thus far. I really believe that I was the least among my friends and family. I never saw myself that way, but that's how they treated me, so I learned to put everyone else before myself. I had to realize what I had been doing. The true power of choice; you can always choose again. Even if you make a mistake, just embrace it and have a chance to learn a valuable lesson. Don't sit around and be hard on yourself; life has more than enough difficult situations. I had to breathe life back into my dreams and pursue it.

Mark 9:23…. Everything is possible for the one who believes.

I dropped the chameleon act and started to live my authentic best life. In singleness! I dropped the fear of fake friends and stood in my truth.

Started speaking my truth instead of keeping it bottled in. I accepted Nakia completely and loved myself with all my heart the way I loved others. I forced myself to answer some questions. I realized that deep down inside, I had this horrible belief. I believed that God placed me on this earth to be rejected, abused, and mistreated by others. I allowed my life to sow the ugliest seed into my mental garden. I had to go back through my life to see when this seed was planted but I had discovered it and I was livid. Jesus died so that we can live life more abundantly. I was the total opposite.

I had been sitting in a mental prison for years. I had this Savior complex where it was somehow my responsibility to make everything right for other people. I was the designated person to make other people happy or help others when they are in trouble. Once I completely saw myself correctly, I quickly took off my cape and set it on fire (this girl is on fire!). I don't know everything, and I don't have to know everything. Other people's problems and opinions no longer dictate my decisions. I demand respect and I don't tolerate disrespect. I no longer have a problem disconnecting from negativity and negative situations. I no longer place myself in situations and circumstances to be around people that do not like me. I don't have to fake it when I have a choice to choose what environment to partake in. Why sit around people that's living a life of hell and torment when you could be sitting in the beautiful garden? It was these realizations that opened up a whole new world for me. I escaped from the world of "I CAN'T" as I entered the world of everything that is POSSIBLE. I am worthy of all things that life has to offer. I spent a lot of time investing in the greatness of others. If I could turn back the hands of time, I would have invested more into myself and less on others.

A Love Letter to Nakia

I am sorry for not always standing up for you. I am sorry for letting you believe that the size and shape of your body reflected the value and beauty of your mind. I am sorry that I didn't stop you from trying to heal your thoughts by bullying your body. I'm sorry that I allowed you to diminish yourself in space when you were already so lovely just as you were. I'm sorry that I didn't tell you that there was never anything wrong with either your mind or your body; I apologize for letting you believe that you were flawed.

I'm sorry I let you think that at times you weren't enough. I'm sorry I let you believe that you needed to change. I am sorry that I didn't tell you that you didn't need to be like anyone else. I'm sorry that I allowed you to be afraid of yourself; to be afraid of living life authentically. I'm so sorry that I let you fear yourself. I'm sorry that I allowed you to believe that your worth was determined by the number of people who liked you and by the grades you received on your report card. I'm sorry you thought that worth was something to be earned. I'm sorry for allowing you to intentionally soften your footprints out of fear of what others would think.

I am sorry that I didn't stop you from hiding in the shadows. I'm sorry I didn't encourage you to instead let your voice be heard. I'm sorry I prevented you from living loudly and freely. I'm sorry I never told you that you were enough, or that you were whole and complete. I'm sorry that I did not remind you that your presence brought infinite beauty and grace into this world. I'm sorry I didn't allow you to love your elegance and light. I'm sorry.

Although it might not seem like much, I can promise you that I am

here now. I promise that I will do my very best to make up for all the
times I didn't take care of you in the ways that I should have. But I do
hope you understand that I was trying; that I never stopped trying. I
always had faith in you, and I always hoped that you would see your
shining light one day. I hope you know that I didn't always trust myself,
and I allowed this uncertainty to taint the way you saw yourself.

I hope you know that I never intentionally put you down or tried to
hurt you. I hope you know that despite how I may have treated you, you
have still lived a beautiful life this far. You have still been compassionate
and courageous and free in your own incredible ways. I hope you know
that no matter what mistakes I made, I will always look back on your life
with nothing but fondness and pride. I am sorry that I allowed you to
listen to whatever others had to say and let them get to you. I am sorry I
pushed you to prove them wrong when you didn't really have to prove
anything in the first place. I understand now that you can never be
perfect because no matter what, you can never please everybody.

I am sorry that I let you be too vulnerable. I am sorry for not allowing
you to be confident in your own skin, and most especially for not letting
you continue writing and thinking about what other people had to say
about the way that you think, speak, and record your experiences. I am
sorry that I have tolerated your thinking that you are not smart enough,
unlike the people around you, making you lose all your motivation and
interest in what you were most passionate about.

I understand now that most of the time, hard work beats talent or
even intelligence. More importantly, who cares if they are smarter, more
attractive, or "better" than you? You are unique, and extraordinary. You
may not be as smart or attractive as they are, but your ability to see
things through, to see the beauty amidst the ugly, makes you just as

amazing.

I now know that I should have just let you go. I should have just permitted you to do whatever you want and imprinted on your mind that it doesn't matter what other people say. It never did, and it never will. What matters is that you are doing something, and that you are never idle. I wish I told you that it is okay to fail and held your hand as you stood up from the fall to start again. No matter how many times, I wish you kept trying. I know that you are capable of anything, and I wish you knew that. I want to turn back time, so I could tell you that if you are not hurting anybody else, not even yourself, you are capable of greatness. You could change the world.

I am sorry I never told you all these things. I do hope that it's not too late to let you know this: Your dream of making a difference in the world is not impossible. Regardless of your age, your gender, who you're with, where you are, and who you are, nothing is impossible. You may have heard that over and over, but it's true. I promise that I will tell you that you are valuable, and that for the most part, I will truly believe it. Even more importantly, I promise that I will treat you like you are valuable. I will treat you like you are worth everything that is wonderful and special in this world.

I'm sorry I let you believe that you needed to change. I am sorry that I didn't tell you that you didn't need to be like anyone else. I'm sorry that I allowed you to be afraid of yourself; to be afraid of living life authentically. I'm so sorry that I let you fear you.

From today on I will raise you up higher than I ever have before, and when you fall down, I will not let you stay down. I will lift you back up, again and again and again.

From today and on, I will support you and value you. From today and
on, I will love you.
From today and on, I will be your friend.

I HAVE – FAITH

I take full accountability for my actions, but what I didn't realize was that I was angry with You, God. I didn't realize that I needed to repent and get it right before it was too late. I had to realize I was using my hurt to sin, playing victim, and blaming God for the delay in my life. The point is that I had character issues that he wanted me to address. God, you allowed demotion in my life to show my heart. I was slow to get the point of how disobedient You allowed car accidents, job loss, miscarriage, dysfunctional relationships, and financial drowning several times. I felt like the plagues of Israel took over my life. There were layers of me that You still needed to uncover.

I discovered a horrible secret about myself. I never dealt with my childhood rejection and feeling unloved. This root was causing me to bear the fruit of desperation and people pleasing. I found myself doing things that I didn't want to do, to keep people from walking out of my life. I was placing people on pedestals and bowing before them, and I was unaware of this behavior. It was only when I became angry that I would be honest with myself about all the times I had to put up with things I didn't like. I would have been able to heal, but I was still lying to myself. Being unhealed in these areas led to obesity. The Holy Spirit showed me I didn't have a weight problem. I was stuffing myself with an emotional problem. I stuffed myself for years.

I courageously pulled myself out of the black hole, so that I could see how far my brokenness went. As a child, I believed my opinions and feelings didn't matter. I was molded to always do what was best for others at the expense of myself. I was conditioned to believe everything was my fault, so I took full responsibility for everything and felt it was my job to always be a problem solver for everyone. There were times I could clearly see that other people were at fault. I was told to shut up, and this created the brokenness of covering up instead of addressing the issues that I saw. My anger wanted justification finally! So, I fell into a trap of blaming others for everything because I was burdened and tired of the load that I was forced to carry as a child.

I moved away from everyone I knew and still found myself still experiencing the same things. I was stuck in a world of victimizing; my family was victimizing me; my so-called friends and coworkers were too. I began to believe God had created me to be abused my whole life. I was stuck in this childish pattern my whole life. Nights I've sat and cried not understanding why me. When God removes everyone from my life, it is just him and I. Time and time again God kept removing people away. That's when I began to fight with God, and the truth was I didn't trust God. God allowed these people to abuse and mistreat me as I pushed myself to seek my purpose. "Why me" turned into "why not me." I realized and became more aware that I was allowing people to treat me in a way that was not in agreement with my truth. I found my voice, and I no longer make excuses for the behavior of others or my own.

Now I think I know it all. Who do I think I am? The only people who get mad at the truth are liars. I let insecure people stop my progress, not seeing that the person might have low self-esteem. Of course, confidence will appear like arrogance to someone who doesn't have any confidence. When people see light in you, they will try to distort what God is trying to do. People did not know it took me years to find my voice and even speak up for myself. The more I learned to use my voice, the more I understood I didn't have to use it as much. I began to hear this constant chatter, and it annoyed me. I realized that I was talking to fill the dead silence from being around boring people. A shift took place and I started standing in silence. As a kid, I talked so much because everyone would just be sitting around looking at each other in silence. I didn't like talking more than others. I just didn't like the feeling of being deaf; life with no sound. I hate talking, and many people don't know that about me. It was never about talking; it was the absence of sound that disturbs me.

Talk about realizing the shift and the people I was begging to love me, to hang out with me, call me, promote me, date me, visit me, accept me - I can't believe how sick I was begging people that I thought I needed, people that I was casting pearls on while they were stepping on them like swine. They despised me because they saw all this greatness and shine on my life. I was so busy focusing on my lack that I was overlooking how truly amazing I am.

I cut distractions and started looking at life like it was an hourglass. No matter what someone tells you, time is our most precious gift, because we can't get that time back once it's wasted. I stopped complaining about things I could not change. I understood that I am enough.

I don't need someone to connect me. I don't need to kiss anyone. I need doors to open for me, and God promised me that he will set forth the path that I shall walk in. I don't need a man to love me. God loves me. God died for me so that I may live.

EPILOGUE

Words to myself…

When God created you, He made no mistakes. You slipped up and allowed others to lead you to believe that you had no purpose. The devil is a lie. You're destined for greatness! You've held onto fear too long. Fear is of the enemy! He didn't create you to have fear in your heart but know that God is always with you even when you think he's not. Now that you have chosen to find your purpose wholeheartedly, your process of transition has started. You now see yourself the way God sees you, not the world or people.

You've been left out and behind for way too long, child. The road I've created for you looks nothing like anyone else's. I have something extra special for you. So, time is of the essence at this moment. Faith is what I know you hold in your heart when I have allowed you to fall at your lowest.

You looked to GOD. You called upon his name. God isn't done with you yet! Your mind can't even begin to fathom what God has for you. Keep pushing towards your destiny! The devil is working overtime because he knows what God's plan is for you. The devil tries to break you over and over, but your faith won't let him. The devil has tried killing you several times. I won't let him. You're my child, God's Child!

Going through this healing process, I have a different outlook on my strengths and weaknesses. One of my biggest strengths is that I know that I need God! I know that without God I am absolutely nothing but with Him I am more than a conqueror. With Him, I am the head and not the tail. I am above and not beneath.

One of my greatest weaknesses is allowing the devil to lead me to believe anything other than God's words, trusting man's word instead of God's, and believing I am anything less than royalty. Healing doesn't have a time limit, but the process is worth it. Stop letting the devil make you afraid to face your situations. Heal by all means necessary. It's lonely but it is worth it.

Sometimes you must hurt in order to know,
Fall in order to grow,
Lose in order to gain,
Because most of life's greatest lessons are learned through pain.